Hymns
Praising Him!
Original Hymns For All Occasions

by Thornton Cline

To access audio visit:
www.halleonard.com/mylibrary

Enter Code
8803-4283-2457-3767

ISBN 978-1-57424-368-0
SAN 683-8022

Cover art by Sylvain Sarrailh

Design by James Creative Group

Copyright © 2018 CENTERSTREAM Publishing
P.O. Box 17878 - Anaheim Hills, CA 92817

www.centerstream-usa.com | centerstrm@aol.com | 714-779-9390

To my loving and generous Aunt Pegge Baughum

Contents

Please note the 12 tracks of the original hymns available online through Hal Leonard are vocal/piano tracks only. They are not fully-produced radio single tracks. There are no recorded sing-along tracks for choirs or vocalists. The vocal/piano recordings are intended to showcase each song's melody, rhythm, phrasing, and harmonies to demonstrate how they would be performed or sung in a live worship service or event where music ministers or worship leaders would lead in simple intimate settings with a choir/voice and piano; or a choir/voice and guitar. These hymns could be performed with a larger group, full worship band, or larger choir.

Preface

Thank you for purchasing this book. I believe you will find it to be helpful in choosing hymns/songs to perform in both contemporary and traditional services, weddings, special services and in concerts. There are 12 new, fresh and original hymns for all occasions.

I am grateful for the opportunity and challenge offered to me by Ron at Centerstream Publishing to write 12 original hymns. I am grateful to my Aunt Pegge Baughum for her genereous gift of her baby grand piano which helped provide much of the inspiration in writing these hymns. I am thankful to James Hunter Welch for his artistic piano performances on the recordings of these hymns. I am grateful to Alice Antimie, Matt Newton and Onisim Antimie for their lovely artistic voice recordings and interpretation of these hymns.

Thank you to my wife, Audrey for her love, belief and support.

Finally, I am grateful to the Lord God Almighty for the inspiration of words and music. If it were not for God, there would be no hymns to sing, nor would there be this hymn book.

Pray My Way Through It

Words and music by
Thornton Cline

2

fall to your knees and thank Him, oh thank Him. And in time, He will lift the

clouds._____ Keep on pray-ing and__ showr-ing Him with_____ praise._____

Wai - ting on Him__ for that bright, sun - ny day. Got to

James 1:2-4 NIV

"Consider it pure joy, my brothers and sisters, whenever you face trials of many kinds, because you know that the testing of your faith produces perseverance. Let perseverance finish its work so that you may be mature and complete, not lacking anything.

I was inspired to write this song after experiencing some challenging and difficult trials. When I read James 1:2-4 (NIV) I realized we are supposed to experience trials in our lives to create maturity and endurance. I realize that nothing is accomplished by worrying. We must pray continually through the storms until we receive answers—until we see the sun shine again.

Blessings Flow

Words and music
by Thornton Cline

cure,____ I can face all my fears. My true source and strength and my

soul pro - vi - der, through your will bless-ings pour out._____Though

trials come and go, Lord you're still in con- trol. Hea-ven's win- dows o- pen wi-der.

Repeat 3 times

Bless-ings flow.__ I give thanks__ for all that you have done.

Malachi 3:10 NIV

"Bring the whole tithe into the storehouse that there may be food in my house. Test me in this" says the Lord Almighty, "and see if I will not throw open the floodgates of Heaven and pour out so much blessing that there will not be enough to store it."

All the blessings God has given me in my life have inspired me to write "Blessings Flow." Blessings come in all forms from receiving God's love, His salvation, His grace and mercy, family and friends, protection, food, clothing and shelter. If we objectively open our eyes, we will see how blessed we are.

Praise You Everywhere

Words and music by
Thornton Cline

Joyful ♩=76

G   Em   C

I sing prai-ses eve-ry-where I go, Eve-ry-thing I see Lord, I

4   Am   D   G   Em   C   SECOND VERSE / LAST TIME

praise you eve-ry-where.__ Praise you in the stars at night, in the new day light. I

8   Am   D   Am(sus4)   G

praise you eve-ry-where I can find you on Sun-days in the pul-pit and the pews.

11 Am(sus4)   G   D

Then a-gain, you're in ma-ny pla-ces, I thought I ne-ver knew, on the

13 Em   C   D   G   Em   C

street, a-round the cor-ner, or as close as my heart. All I have to do is look a-round me. You're

Verse 2

16 D   D⁷   Am(sus4)   G

ne-ver ve-ry far.__ Call your name in a-ny place, a-ny where. It's

19 Am(sus4)   G   D

com-for-ting to know you hear me in my thoughts and prayers. I can

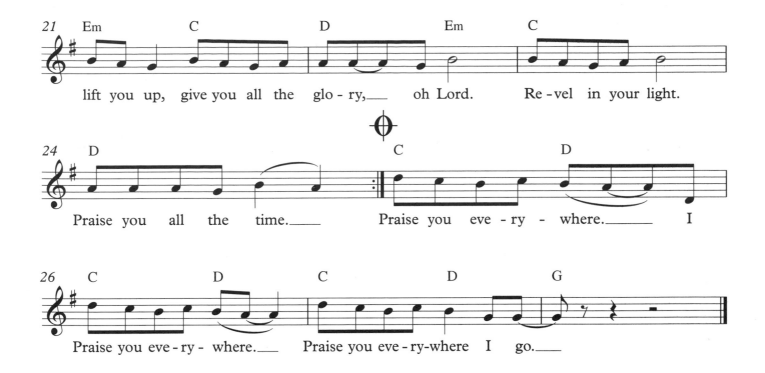

lift you up, give you all the glo - ry,___ oh Lord. Re - vel in your light.

Praise you all the time.___ Praise you eve - ry - where._____ I

Praise you eve - ry - where.___ Praise you eve - ry - where I go.___

Psalm 139:7-12 NIV

"Where can I go from your spirit? Where can I flee from your presence? If I go up to the heavens, you are there; if I make my bed in the depths, you are there. If I rise on the ways of the dawn, settle on the far side of the sea, even there your hand will guide me, your right hand will hold me fast. If I say, "surely the darkness will hide me, and the light become night around me," even the darkness will not be dark to you," the night will shine like day, for darkness is as light to you.

I was moved to write this song, "Praise You Everywhere" after realizing how accessible our God is. God isn't just available in church on Sunday mornings. God can be reached through prayer anytime, anywhere, no matter where we go. He is as close as our hearts.

My Gratitude

Words and music by
Thornton Cline

Psalm 100:4-5 (NIV)

"Enter his gates with thanksgiving and his courts with praise; give thanks to him and praise his name. For the Lord is good and his love endures forever; his faithfulness continues through all generations."

I believe that being thankful to God is a vital and necessary part of worship. We must thank God for our blessings before we can ask Him for anything else. This belief of gratitude led me to write "My Gratitude".

This Is Our Covenant

Words and music by
Thornton Cline

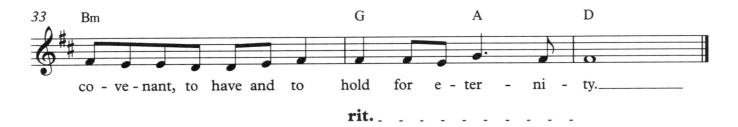

Matthew 19:6 (NIV)

"So they are no longer two, but one flesh. Therefore what God has joined together, let no one separate."

My own marriage has been an inspiration for writing "This is Our Covenant". I realize how serious the marriage covenant is and that the marriage between a man and a woman is a sacred and lasting covenant entered into with and before God.

The Measure of True Love

Words and music by
Thornton Cline

go to the ends of the earth_ with no-thing asked in re - turn._____ I

D.S. 𝄋

ne-ver knew a love could go so high and so deep,_ un - til you showed me_____the

Ne-ver end-ing, al - ways bend-ing, ne-ver gi-ving too much._ That's the mea-sure

of__ true love_____. That's the mea-sure of__ true love_____.

rit. _ _ _ - _ - _ - -

1 Corinthians 13:4-6 (NIV)

"Love is patient, love is kind. It does not envy, it does not boast, it is not proud. It does not dishonor others, it is not self-seeking, it is not easily angered, it keeps no recorded wrongs. Love does not delight in evil but rejoices with the truth."

There are various forms of love. Some are used loosely, masquerading around as so called "love". They are counterfeits. I realized that true love never fails. It is patient, kind and is selfless. That kind of love is rare to find in today's world. This is the inspiration behind "The Measure of True Love".

Today And Forever

Words and music by
Thornton Cline

2

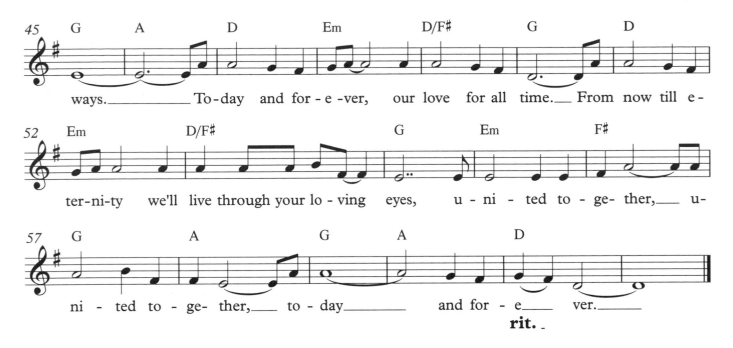

ways._____ To-day and for - e -ver, our love for all time.__ From now till e-

ter-ni-ty we'll live through your lo - ving eyes, u - ni - ted to - ge- ther,__ u-

ni - ted to - ge- ther,__ to - day_____ and for - e__ ver._____

rit. _

Hebrews 13:8 (NIV)

"Jesus Christ is the same yesterday, today and forever."

This Bible verse influenced me to write "Today and Forever" primarily as a wedding song. When we give our promise to someone in holy matrimony, it is in front of God, and Jesus as our witnesses. Nothing changes from the first day we unite together, nor does anything change after we leave this earth. We continue to follow God's never-changing laws and commandments. Sometime man's laws on Earth change and don't seem to be in line with God's laws. Jesus Christ is the same yesterday, today and always.

Joined In Heaven

Words and music
by Thornton Cline

♩=96 Confidently

Joined on Earth, joined in Hea-ven. Two hearts and souls be-come one. Joined to-ge-ther

man and wo-man. With the Fa-ther and the Son Joined on Earth, joined in Hea-ven, through

God's un-con-di-tio-nal love. To the love. We're in world we seem like two un-like-ly

kind. But God's love's wor-king out our dif-feren-ces. We're des-tined to fol-low God's

plans, on our life-time jour-ney from here to e-ter-ni-ty.___ We stand be-fore you on

sa-cred_ ground with our_ pro-mi-ses and vows. sepa-ra-ble,

no-thing can come bet-ween us.___ Though the years might bring us_ trials.

God's love and strength can o-ver-come it all. There is-n't a-ny-thing we can't

do. We stand be - fore you on__ sa - cred__ ground, with our pro - mi - ses and vows. God's un - con - di - tio - nal love.

rit. _

Mark 10:9 (NIV)

"Therefore, what God has joined together, let no one separate."

God has united a man and woman together in love through holy matrimony on Earth as well as in Heaven. That holy union is sacred and is not to be separated here on Earth. This is the inspiration for "Joined in Heaven".

The Cross Changed Everything

Words and music
by Thornton Cline

Passionate ♩=76

The world was dark and void. Sin was ruled by law._ No-one to for-give us_ No a-
tone-ment for our sins. They hun-gered for some-one_who could turn the o-ther cheek. No
eye for eye, on-ly for-give-ness, writ-ten in-to a new law. Hope for e-ter-nal life.
When they cru-ci-fied you._ The cross changed eve-ry-thing. When they
nailed you to that tree. You sa-cri-ficed your bo-dy and blood. You
rose to give us e-ter-ni-ty. The cross changed eve-ry-thing_ through your
grace and mer-cy we are saved. It's some-thing we can't earn. All we have to do is ask._The
world is so much bright-er. We have a ri-sen Sa-vior._ You

show the world there's no-one like you, a hea-ler and the mi-ra-cle man. The pro-mise of sal-va-tion, the gift of e-ter-nal life. The world was dark and void. Sin was ruled by law. No-one to for-give us,___ no a-tone-ment for our sins. Hope for e-ter-nal life. When they cru-ci-fied you._

rit. _ _ _

Galatians 2:19-20 (NIV)

"For through the law I died to the law so that I might live for God. I have been crucified with Christ and I no longer live, but Christ lives in me. The life I now live in the body, I live forth in the Son of God, who loved me and gave himself for me."

I am amazed how the old law was put to rest by the death and resurrection of Jesus Christ. Jesus gave us a new law of forgiveness. He gave us a new life, grace, mercy and salvation---all because of the cross. This inspired me to write "The Cross Changed Everything".

Commune With Me

Words and music
by Thornton Cline

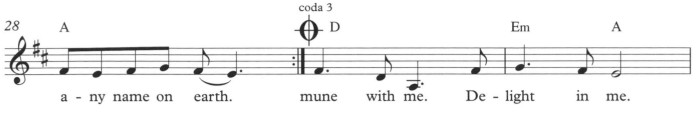

Mark 12:30-31 (NIV)

Love the Lord your God with all your heart and with all your soul and with all your mind and with all your strength.

When we truly love God and Jesus with all our hearts, souls, minds and strength, we are communing with them. This shutting out all the busyness of this world and focusing only of God and Jesus (without interruptions or distractions) in prayer, worship, communication, and listening honors and pleases God. It is a difficult task for most people to truly shut out the world around them. This powerful but necessary concept is the inspiration for "Commune with Me".

Beautiful Baby

Words and music
by Thornton Cline

Adorning ♩ = 62

Beau-ti-ful ba - by._____ Ly-ing in a man - ger._____ It was a

mi-ra-cle_ to see. Who would have i - ma - gined,___ you would be_

king of kings,_____ by the hum-ble life_ you led. Beau-ti-ful ba - by._

___ Shi-ning in swad-dling clothes._____ Bea-ming with your fa__ ther's

love. Beau-ti-ful ba - by,_____ a love that was_ so much more. A grea-ter

love to die_____ for. You were no or - di - na - ry ba-by. You_

healed the sick through the po - wer in your hands. Fed the crowd with five

loaves and two fish. Walked on wa-ter_ as if it_ were land._____ Beau-ti-ful

ba - by.___ A-dorned with fran-kin - cense and myrrh,___ crowned with

thorns on__ a cross. In all your glo-ry rose,___ on that pic-ture per- fect

morn, to give the world ra-di-ant hope. You were King of Kings._____

rit.

James 1:17 (NIV)

"Every good and perfect gift is from above, coming down from the Father of the heavenly lights, who does not change like shifting shadows."

Luke 2:6-14

"While they were there (Mary and Joseph), the time came for the baby to be born, and she gave birth to her firstborn, a son. She wrapped him in cloths and placed him in a manger, because there was no guest room available for them. And there were shepherds living out in the fields nearby, keeping watch over their flocks at night. An angel said to them, "Do not be afraid, I bring you good news that will cause great joy for all the people. Today in the town of David a Savior has been born to you; he is the Messiah, the Lord. This will be a sign to you: You will find a baby wrapped in cloths and lying in a manger." Suddenly a great company of the heavenly host appeared with the angel, praising God and saying, "Glory to God in the highest heaven, and on earth peace to those on whom his favor rests."

"Beautiful Baby" was written one day after reflecting on the two above scripture verses. I can only imagine how magnificent that night must have been, getting to see someone so great as Jesus, the King of Kings for the first time shining in that manager. What a glorious sight to see!

What Would Christmas Be

Words and music by
Thornton Cline

woudn't be Christ-mas at all.___ What would Christ-mas be with-out the an___ gels? What would Christ-mas be with-out dear Ma — ry?___ What would Christ - mas be with- out the Sa - vior.___ It would - n't be Christ - mas at all.___ _____ It would-n't be Christ - mas at all.

rit. _ - - - - - - - - - - - - -

John 14:9 (NIV)

Jesus answered: "Don't you know me, Philip, even after I have been among you such a long time? Anyone who has seen me has seen the Father. How can you say, 'Show us the Father?'

1 Corinthians 15:56-57

"The sting of death is sin, and the power of sin is the law. But thanks be to God! He gives us the victory through our Lord Jesus Christ."

This inspiration to write "What Would Christmas Be" came from the troubling question of what would the world be like if Jesus had never been born? I thought it through, read scriptures and prayed about it. The song "What Would Christmas Be" asks the listeners profound questions on what Christmas would be like. Would we even celebrate it? Perhaps it would be celebrated in the secular sense with Santa Claus. But, if Jesus had never been born, there would be no angels, no baby Jesus, no star, no manager, no wise men, no shepherds and no Mary and Joseph. It would be a world void of hope, salvation and forgiveness. That would be a sad world indeed.

Biographies

Thornton Cline, author/songwriter

Grammy and Dove nominated, twice *Songwriter of the Year, Platinum Certified* and *Maxy Literary Award*-winning author and songwriter, Thornton Cline has had over 150 of his songs recorded by Engelbert Humperdinck, Gloria Gaynor, Ray Peterson, The Manhattans, Rebecca Holden, Gary Puckett, Matt Newton, Tammy Trent, Tim Murphy and in film/television. Cline has had many original choral and instrumental works published by Centerstream, Hal Leonard, Bourne Company, Music 70 Music Publishers, Alfred Music, and Lawson Gould Publishers. Cline has had over 18 children and adult books published by Centerstream, Hal Leonard, Black Rose Writing, and Indigo Sea Publishers. He is represented by literary agent, Paul Shepherd. Cline gives all the glory and honor to God who gave him the gift of writing songs, books and his debut hymn/song book.

Alice Antimie, singer, recording artist, illustrator and writer

Alice Antimie is originally from Anaheim California but has lived in Music City for almost two decades now. Alice grew up in a musical family and has been involved in her local church choir and worship ministry since she was 11. Alice's passion for singing and songwriting has followed her over the years through difficult times but also joyful times. Alice plans to continue singing and writing music and hopes to release some original songs sometime soon. Antimie's voice can be heard singing on the recordings of Thornton Cline's debut hymn/song book.

Onisim Antimie, vocal recording artist

Onisim Antimie, also from Anaheim, California, has been in the music scene for as long as he could remember. Coming from a family of musically inclined individuals, Onisim was exposed to the love of music early on. Onisim has been in choir and band since he was able to join. He started his musical career by playing trumpet in his church band. Later on, he expanded his involvement by participating in his school and church choir, as well as learning to play the piano. Onisim plans to continue working with music, but knows that whichever route life takes him, the music will always be there.

Matt Newton, artist, and songwriter

Matt Newton grew up in Washington, Indiana. He has been a professional singer for the last 25 years. He has concertized all over the world in countless venues and vocal styles. He has been considered for two Grammy Award nominations. His voice can be heard on the holiday hit, "Catch a Snowflake" written by Grammy nominated songwriter, Thornton Cline. The song continues to be a worldwide hit. When Matt is not singing, he is a certified archery instructor and founder of Archers on International Missions, a non-profit organization using archery to lead the world to Christ.

James Hunter Welch, pianist, recording artist and worship leader

James Hunter Welch was born and currently resides in his hometown of Lebanon, Tennessee. He has been a vital part of multiple ensembles, orchestras, and bands in the Middle Tennessee area while playing a variety of styles, including jazz, contemporary, and classical. His music mentors who selflessly gave their time to teach him theory and technique include Tony Cook, Carolyn Blake and Joyce Roseman. James gives God his Father all the credit and honor for his musical ability. He currently serves in the music ministry at Crossroads Fellowship in Lebanon, Tennessee.

Credits

God

Pegge Baughum

Audrey, Alex and Mollie Cline

Roberta Cline

Ron Middlebrook and Centerstream Publishing

Hal Leonard

James Hunter Welch

Alice Antimie

Onisim Antimie

Matt Newton

Lacie Carpenter

Hendersonville Christian Academy

Lawrence Boothby, photographer

Marcelo Cataldo, transcriber

Clinetel Music